SUPERNATURAL
JOIN THE HUNT

TAROT GUIDEBOOK

WRITTEN BY **MINERVA SIEGEL**

ART BY **MATTHEW SKIFF**

TITAN
BOOKS
LONDON

CONTENTS

57
THE MINOR ARCANA

115
TAROT READINGS

INTRODUCTION

From its very beginning, *Supernatural* has been a show rich in mythology, folklore, and symbolism. So much more than a simple horror series, *Supernatural*'s multilayered story pulls from epic traditions around the globe, touching on some of the biggest themes in fiction: life, death, fate versus free will, and above all, family. While the show has included many fascinating, complex, and beloved characters over the years, it has remained, for the most part, the story of Sam and Dean Winchester: two brothers destined, over and over again, to save the world.

Designed for both experienced tarot readers and those new to the practice, the *Supernatural* Tarot Deck reimagines the iconic characters and artifacts of *Supernatural* as traditional tarot cards, telling the story of the Winchesters through the classic ancient symbolism. The journey you're about to plunge into will take you far beyond fortune-telling; you'll soon find yourself on a powerful path of self-discovery, leading through Heaven, Hell, Purgatory, and beyond. Stay vigilant, watch out for monsters, and enjoy the ride.

Though the words *tarot reading* may conjure mental images of mystical psychics like Missouri Moseley or intimidating, regal witches like Rowena MacLeod, tarot can be used for so much more than fortune-telling. With its rich symbolism, archetypal figures, and overarching themes, tarot can be a valuable tool for honing intution and facilitating personal growth. Reading the cards can offer profound insight into the complicated and varied influences that appear throughout our lives, revealing hidden truths and helping us make confident choices as we continue on our individual roads. Whether you're in search of a conventional apple-pie life or you're looking to embrace a grand, transformative adventure, tarot can help you figure out where you want to go and how to get there.

Each card in the *Supernatural* Tarot Deck utilizes a carefully chosen character, theme, or scene from the show to illustrate the traditional meaning of the card. In the Guidebook, interpretations of each tarot card are given for both the upright and reversed card orientations. The final chapter includes *Supernatural*-inspired tarot spreads to get you started on your journey.

So pack up your Impala, and prepare to embark on an exciting adventure filled with cryptic warnings, mystical symbolism, sage advice, and . . . pie. Don't forget the pie.

UNDERSTANDING YOUR TAROT DECK

There are 78 cards in a tarot deck, and each one has a different meaning depending on whether it's drawn in its upright or reversed (upside-down) position. The deck is divided into two sets of cards: the Major Arcana and the Minor Arcana. The Major Arcana comprises 22 cards, numbered 0 to XXI. These cards represent impactful situations with long-lasting effects and major life themes. They chronologically tell the exciting and perilous story of The Fool, or in the case of the *Supernatural* Tarot Deck, Fools, who appear on the first card in the Major Arcana, numbered 0. In the *Supernatural* Tarot Deck, The Fool card is represented by Sam and Dean Winchester as they start their harrowing journey to discover their destiny.

The remaining 56 cards in a tarot deck are called the Minor Arcana. They represent everyday situations, personalities, and life themes with short-term effects. The Minor Arcana are evenly divided into four suits. In the *Supernatural* Tarot Deck, the suits are Bones, Pentagrams, Blades, and Goblets, which are

THE FOOLS

VI · THE LOVERS ·

representative of the traditional tarot suits of Wands, Pentacles, Swords, and Cups, respectively.

The suit of Bones corresponds to the element Fire. Cards of this suit represent ideas, inspiration, passion, and ambition.

The suit of Pentagrams corresponds to the element Earth and deals with the physical world, material objects and possessions, work, money, deals, and the home.

The suit of Blades corresponds to the element Air. Cards of this suit have to do with intellect, knowledge, personal beliefs, change, action, and conflict.

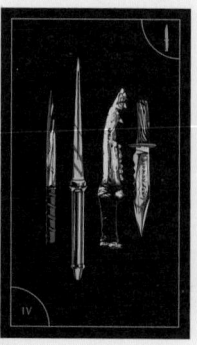 

The suit of Goblets corresponds to the element Water. These cards represent emotions, intuition, relationships, friendships, and other personal connections.

Each of these 4 suits contains 14 cards, including 4 unnumbered court cards: the Page, Knight, Queen, and King. Court cards symbolize personality types, behavior patterns, and sometimes, actual people in your life. The remaining cards in each suit are numbered I (Ace) to X.

THE
MAJOR
ARCANA

THE FOOLS

The Fool represents the very beginning of an important new journey or major life change. Sam and Dean Winchester's transition into solo hunters after their father's disappearance perfectly embodies the spirit of The Fool tarot card.

UPRIGHT: You're on the verge of a grand new adventure. While you may not be able to fully see all the twists and turns (or monsters, magic, and demons) awaiting you on this new path, have faith in its importance. Remember why you started this journey; it will carry you through to success.

REVERSED: The Fool reversed comes as a warning against impulsive action. Plan your next moves carefully to avoid getting caught up in a messy predicament. Even if you do find yourself trapped, remember all's not lost. Like Sam and Dean, there will be friends and allies along the way to help you through thick and thin, come what may.

THE FOOLS

I · THE MAGICIAN

I

THE MAGICIAN

Just as Chuck is the ultimate source of almighty creative power, the wielder of the pen, God himself, The Magician tarot card is a reminder to embrace your own infinite potential.

UPRIGHT: The Magician is full of inspired action. You are the writer of your own story, and you can manifest the future you want for yourself if you concentrate and put decisive action and momentum behind your creative vision.

REVERSED: Have you been doubting yourself lately? Reversed, The Magician becomes unsure of what steps to take next. Don't rush yourself. Take a break, and trust in the process. You'll feel inspired to step back into your full power soon.

II

THE HIGH PRIESTESS

The High Priestess, like Rowena, is a very powerful, magical figure who is known to have a lot going on beneath the surface.

UPRIGHT: The High Priestess as a tarot card advises you to trust your intuition. Just as Rowena is able to regain power time after time, The High Priestess is adept at overcoming obstacles. Listen to your instincts, dig deep to find your strength, and keep going.

REVERSED: Rowena is a master manipulator and ruthless in the pursuit of what she wants. Beware of getting caught up in someone else's scheme. Are you sure you're seeing things as they really are? Now is not the time to ignore your gut feelings. If something doesn't feel quite right to you, it probably isn't.

II · THE HIGH PRIESTESS

III · THE EMPRESS

III

THE EMPRESS

The Empress is a powerful, protective, and nurturing maternal figure, much like the Winchester matriarch, Mary.

UPRIGHT: The Empress tarot card advises you to lead with compassion. You'll succeed faster if you nurture and guide others rather than bully and try to force them into doing what you want them to.

REVERSED: When Mary is brought back to life after being dead for thirty-three years, she finds herself over-whelmed and realizes she needs to go her own way for a while in order to find herself again. Reversed, The Empress tarot card comes as a call to rediscover your center and get back in touch with your own truth.

IV

THE EMPEROR

The Emperor is the ultimate authoritarian, a strong patriarchal figure, much like master hunter John Winchester.

UPRIGHT: John is a skilled and knowledgeable hunter, and his thorough record keeping helps his sons when they find his journal and decide to follow in his footsteps. The Emperor advises you to stay vigilant, sensible, and disciplined.

REVERSED: You're feeling maxed out and burdened by responsibilities, so it's time to reevaluate your routines. Analyze the way you spend your energy, and restructure the parts of your life that feel overwhelming.

IV · THE EMPEROR

V · THE HIEROPHANT

V

THE HIEROPHANT

The Hierophant respects and values tradition, order, and rules, much like Billie, a reaper, and later the new Death, who takes her role as keeper of the natural order very seriously.

UPRIGHT: The Hierophant tarot card advises you to put order to chaos using time-honored structures and traditions. Now isn't the time for rebellion and questioning the status quo. Showing respect for established institutions and hierarchies will benefit you in the long run.

REVERSED: When The Hierophant comes forward reversed, it symbolizes the need to shake up traditions and question the rules. Ask yourself if conformity is serving you well or holding you back. Don't be afraid to blaze your own trail and create a path that works better for you.

VI

THE LOVERS

When Sam's girlfriend Jessica is killed, Sam is faced with what is arguably the biggest decision of his life: He must decide whether to avenge her death by becoming a hunter or to choose a normal human life. The Lovers tarot card symbolizes a major life decision or crossroad.

UPRIGHT: The Lovers is a tarot card depicting a harmonious union, friendship, or partnership. However, within this partnership, there is an important choice to be made. When you find yourself faced with a life-changing decision, The Lovers tarot card advises you to listen to your heart.

REVERSED: When The Lovers tarot card shows up reversed in a reading, it suggests a partnership in your life has soured. Things aren't as harmonious and easy as they should be. It's time to step back and reevaluate the situation. Can this partnership be fixed, or is it time to move on?

VI · THE LOVERS

VII · THE CHARIOT

VII

THE CHARIOT

The Chariot symbolizes forward momentum, willpower, drive, and triumph. In *Supernatural*, the Winchester's chariot is Dean's inherited 1967 Chevrolet Impala, the car that carries them through the many trials and triumphs of their journey.

UPRIGHT: Sam and Dean have a firm belief in their moral convictions and the importance of their job each time they set out on one. The Chariot suggests you take a leaf out of their book and go after your goals with determination and courage. Even if you can't quite see where this new road leads, your confidence will ensure you're triumphant.

REVERSED: The Chariot reversed symbolizes the sense of being trapped or powerless. Have you been feeling directionless or out of control? Take time to ground yourself and rediscover your center. Trust in your own potential. You're more capable than you give yourself credit for.

VIII

STRENGTH

The tarot card Strength represents the inner resolve required to take control of your own destiny, much like Dean's vampire friend Benny, whose tragic arc forces him to make difficult choices over and over again.

UPRIGHT: Benny rejects his vampire maker, the woman he loves, and even his own bloodthirsty nature in an effort to live a life that harms no one. Strength advises you to follow your heart and pursue the path that feels right to you rather than the one that seems easier or expected.

REVERSED: When the Strength tarot card is drawn reversed, it's a sign there are outside forces causing trouble for you and your plans. Identify who or what is making your life difficult, and rely on your instincts when deciding how to deal with these obstacles. You have what it takes to come out of this on top. Trust your intuition.

VIII · STRENGTH

IX · THE HERMIT

IX

THE HERMIT

The Hermit, like Bobby Singer, is a solitary guide who has a talent for illuminating the truth and bringing out the best in people.

UPRIGHT: The Hermit is a call to look inward. Take a break from the hustle and bustle of the outside world, and make time for self-reflection. A period of introspection will enable you to approach things with greater clarity.

REVERSED: The Hermit, when reversed, indicates you've been avoiding something important. Maybe you're not ready to face the truth about a situation just yet, but deep down, you know what's really going on. Denial won't make things better. Follow Bobby's example and bravely seek the truth. Things will turn out for the best.

X

THE WHEEL OF FORTUNE

The Wheel of Fortune represents a twist of fate or major change in luck, such as the ones brought on by the legendary lucky rabbit's foot, which showers the person who posesses it with an amazing spree of good fortune . . . until they lose it.

UPRIGHT: The main theme of The Wheel of Fortune is that what goes around comes around. The rabbit's foot brings good luck to its owner, but when it falls out of their possession, the former owner is cursed with bad luck. This cyclical nature of fortune and fate can serve as both a hopeful reminder and a warning. Enjoy and appreciate the good times, and remember the bad ones won't last forever.

REVERSED: The momentum of The Wheel of Fortune is stalled when reversed. You're stagnant, stuck, or digging in your heels, refusing to move forward. Instead of fearing change, embrace it to make transitions go more smoothly.

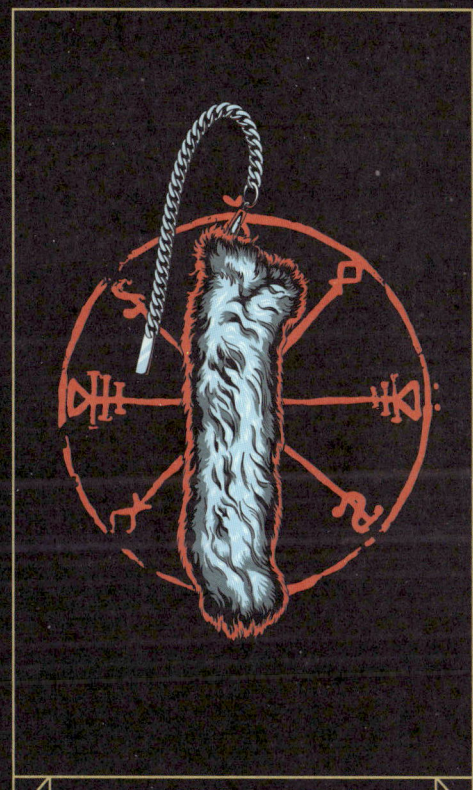

X · THE WHEEL
OF FORTUNE

XI · JUSTICE

XI

JUSTICE

Sheriff Donna Hanscum is a fair and just officer of the law, with a strong moral compass, which is the basis for the Justice tarot card.

UPRIGHT: After learning the truth about the existence of monsters, Donna commits to becoming a hunter under Jody Mills's tutelage. The tarot card Justice advises you to check in with your own moral compass, and make sure you're acting in accordance with your values.

REVERSED: Justice indicates that a major situation, power dynamic, or relationship in your life has become unbalanced and unfair—much like Donna's relationship with her ex-husband. This tarot card advises you to make sure you're valuing yourself and getting what you're owed, and that you're treating others fairly in return.

XII

THE HANGED MAN

Castiel's identity as a rigid, detached, loyal soldier of
Heaven is forever changed as he forms a close relationship with the Winchester brothers. Such major shifts
in perspective are embodied perfectly in the spirit of
The Hanged Man.

UPRIGHT: This tarot card heralds important realizations
and epiphanies. Change can be difficult, but being
open to new ideas and perspectives can serve you well.
It may even help you prevent the apocalypse.

REVERSED: The Hanged Man reversed indicates an
important situation in your life is currently on hold or
not progressing in the way you were hoping for. If you
feel things are stuck in limbo, reevaluate your strategy
to come up with an alternative route to your goal.

XII · THE HANGED MAN

XIII

DEATH

Death the Horseman is an ancient being who plays an important role in preserving the natural order by instigating the transition from life to afterlife. Death as a tarot card symbolizes the inevitable nature of important transformations.

UPRIGHT: You're going through a transition that will ultimately have a big impact on your life. Change can sometimes be a challenging process, but trust the outcome will be worth it.

REVERSED: Are you resisting a change you know is inevitable? Reversed, the transformation symbolized by the Death tarot card is stalled. While it's natural to fear change, delaying the process won't do you any favors. Be brave, and move forward.

XIII · DEATH

XIV · TEMPERANCE

XIV

—

TEMPERANCE

Sheriff Jody Mills is a woman who smoothly inhabits many different roles in her life. She is a successful career woman, a fierce hunter, and a strong, protective mother to her foster kids. She is a perfect embodiment of Temperance, a card which symbolizes levelheadedness, fairness, and good judgment and reminds us to cultivate balance and moderation in our lives.

UPRIGHT: Temperance is a reminder of the importance of sensibility, staying calm in stressful situations, and taking the middle road. There are times when battling things out is necessary, but sometimes, approaching situations with calm, practical sensibility will yield better results.

REVERSED: Temperance reversed is a reminder to take care of practical matters. Make sure the mundane aspects of life are in order before setting off on your next great adventure (or monster-hunting trip). Paying attention to the details may feel tedious and boring, but it will set you up for success.

XV · THE DEVIL

XV

THE DEVIL

The Devil is a warning against corruption, overindulgence, and egotism, traits the fallen angel Lucifer has in abundance.

UPRIGHT: Lucifer is arrogant, egotistical, and ruthless in his pursuit of revenge against God. He feels victimized and uses this as a justification to hurt others. The Devil tarot card indicates you're being blinded by that sort of single-mindedness, and as a result, you're allowing yourself to remain chained to your negative thought patterns and actions. Take a step back, look at the big picture, and consider the consequences of your actions.

REVERSED: Lucifer is an immensely powerful fallen archangel, but even he needs the permission of a human to use them as a vessel. When The Devil tarot card is reversed, it's a reminder that even when you feel powerless, you do ultimately have control over your own destiny. You can escape your devil if you can find the courage to break your chains and send him on his way.

XVI

THE TOWER

The Tower represents a powerful destruction, like the calamity caused by the release of the Darkness, God's sister Amara. While this sort of chaos is often initially perceived as negative, the destruction ultimately leads to new beginnings, which can represent an important step on your overall life path.

UPRIGHT: The Tower heralds a collapse of an existing structure or system. Whatever unforeseen twist of fate this may represent in your life, it is sure to shake things up in a major way. While this change can be rattling, it's necessary and inevitable. Trust that everything will turn out all right in the end.

REVERSED: The Tower reversed indicates you're resisting a major change in your life. You know what needs to happen but are refusing to acknowledge the truth. Accepting the reality of the situation, even if it's difficult, will ultimately benefit you more than denial will.

XVI · THE TOWER

XVII · THE STAR

XVII

THE STAR

The Star represents hope, possibility, and purity. Though Jack Kline is the son of Lucifer himself, he takes charge of his own destiny and chooses to fight against evil. An innocent being in a world of monsters, he embodies the innate goodness of The Star.

UPRIGHT: Even when it seems as though the odds are stacked against you, The Star is a reminder to have hope. You don't have to accept a life you don't want. Remember, you have more power and control over your future than you think you do. Embrace it.

REVERSED: When reversed, the hopeful energy of The Star turns to disappointment. Things haven't turned out the way you had hoped they would. Let yourself process this recent turn of events, but don't despair. There is still hope in The Star, even when it's reversed. There are more opportunities for you on the horizon.

XVIII

THE MOON

Gabriel is the ultimate trickster, a master of illusion. The Moon represents deception, hidden agendas, and the idea that nothing is ever what it seems.

UPRIGHT: The Moon indicates there's more going on than meets the eye. Things aren't what they seem to be at first glance, so stay vigilant and analyze situations carefully to figure out what's really going on. The Moon tarot card suggests you trust your intuition and investigate any hunches or gut feelings you may have.

REVERSED: The Moon reversed represents worry, paranoia, and fear—but are these feelings based in reality, or are you letting anxiety get the best of you? Take a deep breath and step back, and look at the situation with fresh eyes to gain a more balanced perspective.

XVIII · THE MOON

XIX

THE SUN

Dean refers to Charlie Bradbury as "the little sister I never wanted." Her playful bond with the Winchester brothers makes her the perfect match for The Sun tarot card, which represents happiness, positivity, and success.

UPRIGHT: The Sun tarot card is a sign of positive things to come and a reminder to stop and enjoy the little things in life. Use proud self-proclaimed "nerd" Charlie as inspiration to embrace whatever makes you happy.

REVERSED: Sometimes even the best-laid plans fail. The Sun reversed indicates sadness and disappointment. Dust yourself off, and carry on. There are more battles to be fought and codes to be cracked!

XIX · THE SUN

XX · JUDGMENT

XX

JUDGMENT

The tarot card Judgment is all about reckoning and atonement. The archangel Michael wishes to bring an end to humanity's time on earth through the Apocalypse but ultimately finds his own awakening when Castiel forces him to confront the truth of God's nature.

UPRIGHT: The message of the Judgment tarot card is loud and clear: What you reap, you sow; the time to sow is now, as one cycle begins to come to an end. Balance intuition with logic to make decisions, and take time to really think through any and all possible repercussions of your actions to avoid regrets later.

REVERSED: Have you been feeling burdened by shame or regret? The Judgment tarot card, when reversed, shows you're feeling self-critical and reflective. Self-analysis can be beneficial if you're proactive about it. Learn from mistakes, and make amends wherever possible, but then forgive yourself and move on.

XXI · THE WORLD

XXI

THE WORLD

The World represents beginnings, endings, and things coming full circle. For the Winchesters, their world is defined by the open road, the setting for their many adventures and the path that carries them to their destiny.

UPRIGHT: There's a cyclical element to The World tarot card. Whether you've just finished a major chapter in your life, or you're revving up your engines and heading out on your next big adventure, remember that life is never stagnant. Enjoy the ride.

REVERSED: The World, reversed, shows a need for closure. There are loose ends that still need to be tied up. You can't move forward without pausing to process and work through whatever is holding you back.

THE
MINOR
ARCANA

SUIT OF BONES

KING OF BONES

UPRIGHT: The King of Bones is an innovative, passionate leader with an independent streak. This tarot card reminds you that your imagination is one of your most valuable assets. Whether you're taking down the Word of God like Metatron or crafting your own brilliant narrative, use your creativity wisely to achieve your goals.

KING OF BONES

REVERSED: Unrealistic, unattainable expectations mar the leadership of the King of Bones. While being a visionary is great, don't lose sight of reality. A bit of pragmatism can go a long way.

QUEEN OF BONES

UPRIGHT: The Queen of Bones is an ambitious, alluring leader who gets what she wants. She loves attention and gets it. Whether you find yourself fighting the Winchesters or facing a more mundane battle, use ingenuity and determination to see you through to victory.

QUEEN OF BONES

REVERSED: Has your confidence recently taken a blow? The Queen of Bones reversed represents someone who has lost their fire. If you're feeling uninspired, reconnect with your passions. Reigniting your spark will help you rediscover your self-confidence.

KNIGHT OF BONES

UPRIGHT: The Knight of Bones, like Eileen Leahy, is both a capable and fierce warrior and a loyal friend. This tarot card advises you to put action behind your visions and goals. Set your sights on a goal, and pursue it with a potent mix of determination and kindness.

KNIGHT OF BONES

REVERSED: When reversed, the energy and motivation of the Knight of Bones turns restless and irritated. If things aren't going according to plan right now, adjust your strategy. Barreling onward will only lead to you becoming frustrated by a continued lack of progress. Pause to rethink the situation, and come up with a more efficient game plan.

PAGE OF BONES

UPRIGHT: Claire Novak is enthusiastic, rebellious, and excited to pursue life as a hunter, which embodies the spirit of the Page of Bones. Though the Page of Bones may have the best intentions, naivety is sometimes a downfall. This tarot card advises you to approach challenges with optimism, while taking care to be aware of possible risks.

PAGE OF BONES

REVERSED: When reversed, the Page of Bones's naivety gives way to immaturity and selfishness. This card can also show a lack of discipline and follow-through. Your goals and aspirations are important, but remember that you have to put action, sensible strategy, and real work into them in order to bring them to life.

ACE OF BONES

UPRIGHT: The Ace of Bones represents the inspired spark of a new creative undertaking. This card is a sign to follow your passions and go all in while pursuing what inspires you.

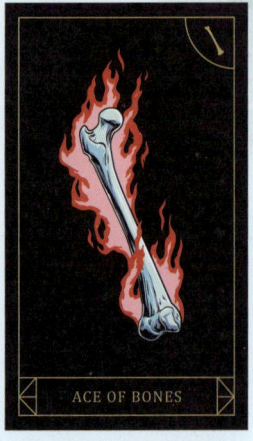

ACE OF BONES

REVERSED: When reversed, the creative energy of the Ace of Bones is blocked, and the reader is left feeling uninspired. Sometimes, this card can also indicate that a creative venture has soured, and it's time to reevaluate and make major adjustments to your original plan.

TWO OF BONES

UPRIGHT: The Two of Bones encourages you to look to the future. Careful planning is more important than making a quick choice right now. Do your research, and focus on coming up with a well-thought-out strategy to set yourself up for success. Sometimes, Two of Bones can indicate travel on the horizon.

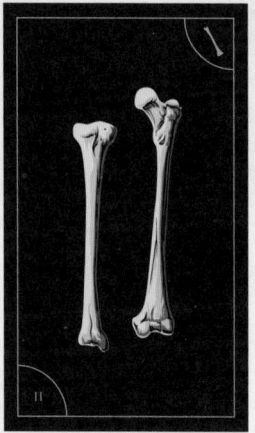

REVERSED: The Two of Bones reversed indicates there's a personal decision to be made, but you're unsure how to proceed. Even though this decision feels overwhelming, logically weighing the pros and cons won't be of much help to you. Look inward for answers, and make the choice that sparks excitement. Even if that road is more difficult, it will be more rewarding.

THREE OF BONES

UPRIGHT: Eve, as the Mother of All Monsters, is a powerful creatrix. She gave life to the great Alpha Monsters, who in turn, procreated and manifested entire species of their kind. Three of Bones represents creation, collaboration, growth, and expansion. Working together with others toward a common goal will lead to impactful, lasting success.

REVERSED: When reversed, the expansive growth indicated by the Three of Bones tarot card isn't being allowed to manifest. You may be playing it safe, afraid to step out of your comfort zone and embrace your full potential. Don't bridle your ambition. Now's the time to set your sights higher, and give it all you've got.

FOUR OF BONES

UPRIGHT: Four of Bones is a tarot card of celebration, success, harmony, and happiness, particularly at home or within the family. It often heralds exciting news relating to major life milestones. When this card comes forward in a tarot reading, it's a positive sign that an exciting announcement is on the way.

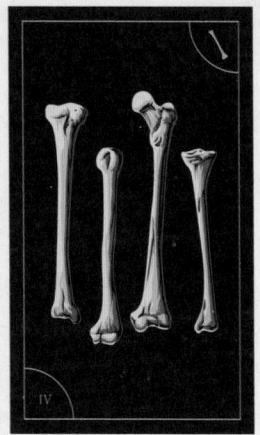

REVERSED: When reversed, the Four of Bones tarot card suggests disharmony and a breakdown in communication at home or among those within your inner circle. There's a lot of tension and unrest. Work on stabilizing your foundation by hearing others out, respecting others' needs, and being open to compromise.

FIVE OF BONES

UPRIGHT: Zachariah is tasked with convincing Dean to allow Michael to use him as his vessel in the great battle against Lucifer. He gets increasingly frustrated, desperate, and cruel as Dean continues to refuse. Zachariah's toxic, manipulative nature and the-end-justifies-the-means persistence personify the Five of Bones tarot card, which represents conflict, unrest, and tension.

REVERSED: When reversed, the discontent signified by the Five of Bones is turned inward. Are you experiencing an internal struggle? Do you feel as though you're at war with yourself? Sometimes, this tarot card can indicate you're avoiding a necessary conflict to your own detriment. Take time to connect with your true feelings, goals, and motivations to move forward with more clarity and focus.

SIX OF BONES

UPRIGHT: Though under-
estimated for his Lynyrd
Skynyrd roadie aesthetic,
Ash gains respect and
admiration by putting his
incredible intellect to
good use time and time
again. Six of Bones signifies this sort of recognition
and achievement. When
this tarot card comes
forward in a reading, it's
your time to shine.

REVERSED: Have you been
letting your ego get the better of you? Reversed, the
Six of Bones tarot card shows overconfidence and
elitism. While it's entirely healthy to be proud of your
accomplishments, take care not to let them go to your
head and cloud your judgment.

SEVEN OF BONES

UPRIGHT: Seven of Bones indicates you're experiencing fierce competition. Perhaps you're battling a rival for a common goal, or perhaps someone in your life is envious of you and looking to usurp your position. This tarot card advises you to bear down and stand your ground. Perseverance and determination will help you come out on top.

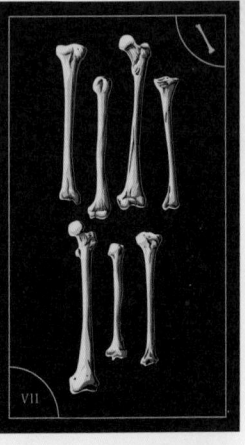

REVERSED: When reversed, the Seven of Bones tarot card shows you've been fighting a hard battle and are feeling discouraged. If you're exhausted and frustrated by a lack of progress, it may be time to cut your losses and move on. Maybe this just wasn't meant to be your win. Trust that better opportunities are in store for you.

EIGHT OF BONES

UPRIGHT: Eight of Bones advises you to embrace inevitable changes and transformations. Sometimes this tarot card can suggest you're heading into a busy, hectic chapter of your life. Rather than getting overwhelmed, things will be easier for you if you go with the flow.

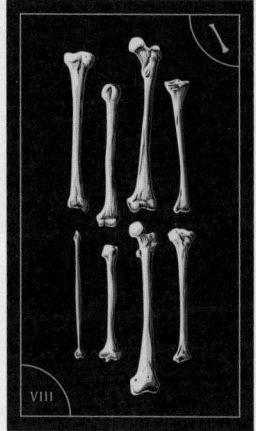

REVERSED: Are you frustrated by obstacles impeding your progress? Eight of Bones reversed indicates delays and blockages. If you're struggling to get where you want to go, accept that this route isn't working for you, and find a new path.

NINE OF BONES

UPRIGHT: The archangel
Raphael fiercely fights to
become the new Ruler of
Heaven after Michael's
defeat. A traditionalist,
he sees this position as
his right. Nine of Bones
advises you to defend and
protect what's yours.
Don't let others come
between you and your
goals. It's time to get clear
on your boundaries and
stick to them.

REVERSED: Nine of Bones reversed suggests you're
feeling unsupported and heavily burdened. With
Michael and Lucifer trapped in the Cage, it's left to
Raphael to free them and get their apocalyptic plans
back on track. If you find yourself feeling overwhelmed
by responsibilities, reevaluate them to prioritize the
ones that are truly most important to you.

TEN OF BONES

UPRIGHT: After helping the Winchesters prevent the apocalypse, Castiel finds himself in the precarious position of trying to secretly collaborate with both the brothers and Crowley, while fighting a civil war in Heaven. Full of doubt, he prays to God to tell him if he's on the right path. Ten of Bones represents the feeling of being exhausted by heavy burdens. This card advises you to make sure the responsibilities you're choosing to take on are really yours to carry.

REVERSED: When reversed, the weight of responsibility represented by the upright Ten of Bones has been lifted. You can finally breathe a little easier with less stress in your life. Often, when this tarot card comes forward in a reading, it's a sign that relief is soon to come. If you're feeling exhausted, know that the end of your troubles is near.

SUIT OF PENTAGRAMS

KING OF PENTAGRAMS

UPRIGHT: Crowley is a slick, power-hungry demon who's always game for a striking good deal. The King of Pentagrams is a shrewd, business-savvy figure who builds a lasting, secure, abundant empire. This tarot card advises you to consider the long-term impact of your decisions and to focus on setting yourself up for future success.

KING OF
PENTAGRAMS

REVERSED: The King of Pentagrams reversed suggests an imbalance in your relationship with wealth. Are sure you're managing your money well? Have you recently gotten too caught up in materialism? Reexamine your relationship with money, and be careful not to let your ego get tied up with your financial status.

QUEEN OF PENTAGRAMS

UPRIGHT: The Queen of Pentagrams, like entrepreneurial fallen angel Anael, is a business-savvy opportunist who appreciates the finer things in life. Anael turns her powers into profits by becoming a faith healer. The Queen of Pentagrams tarot card advises you to embrace your inner pragmatism to create abundance in your life.

REVERSED: While the upright Queen of Pentagrams suggests the cultivation of material abundance, reversed, this tarot card advises you to cultivate an inner wealth. Focus on self-care now. Recognizing and nurturing your emotional and spiritual needs will put you in the balanced frame of mind needed to manifest physical success.

KNIGHT OF PENTAGRAMS

UPRIGHT: Azazel is a single-minded, throughly evil Prince of Hell who will stop at nothing to achieve his goal of freeing Lucifer. The Knight of Pentagrams advises you to put action behind your goals, especially ones relating to your career or finances. You have big dreams, and now's the time to go after them.

KNIGHT OF PENTAGRAMS

REVERSED: The Knight of Pentagrams reversed indicates the momentum on a situation relating to your career or income has stalled. It could be a business venture isn't as fruitful as was anticipated, or maybe you're not getting ahead at work. If you find yourself feeling unsuccessful, it may be time to pivot. Alter your strategies, or reexamine your goals to make sure you're spending your time and energy in ways that will really benefit you in the long run.

PAGE OF PENTAGRAMS

UPRIGHT: The Page of Pentagrams tarot card represents the beginning of a new business venture. Ed and Harry turn their passion for paranormal investigation into a new business by starting their show, *Ghostfacers*. The Page of Pentagrams encourages you to think about how you can use your own unique interests and skill set to create

profit. Sometimes this tarot card suggests a new job or business opportunity will present itself to you soon.

REVERSED: Have you been feeling unmotivated? Unsure how to make progress in your career or manifest more money? The Page of Pentagrams reversed indicates you may not be spending your time in the ways that will ultimately benefit you the most. If you've lost your passion for your job, it may be time to think about making a change in your professional life. Consider taking a new class or signing up for an inspiring seminar to spark your fire again.

ACE OF PENTAGRAMS

UPRIGHT: The Ace of Pentagrams represents professional opportunities, new beginnings related to the home, and positive changes in your finances. Now's the time to begin something new, because this tarot card is a positive sign that any endeavors you choose to undertake have the potential to create abundance in your life.

ACE OF
PENTAGRAMS

REVERSED: When reversed, the affirmative message of the upright Ace of Pentagrams becomes negative. The card in this orientation suggests a new project you're planning may not be successful. Don't be discouraged! Instead, try to find a different way to reach your goal. Just because this particular path may not be right for you doesn't mean there isn't a path that is—you just have to find it.

TWO OF PENTAGRAMS

UPRIGHT: While trying to escape Abbadon, Sam and Dean's grandfather, Henry Winchester, ends up traveling through time from 1958 to 2013. He struggles with the decision of whether or not to return to his original time, knowing that doing so could alter reality. The Two of Pentagrams indicates you're being faced with a tough decision, especially relating to your family or finances. This card advises you that finding balance will be the key to your success.

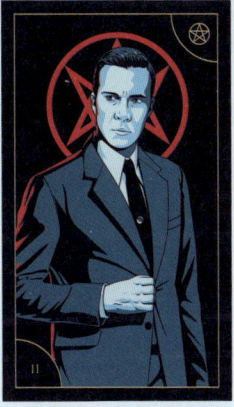

REVERSED: The Two of Pentagrams reversed indicates an imbalance between your home and professional lives. Have you been focusing the majority of your attention on one aspect of your life, to the detriment of the other? Reflect on how you're spending your time, and make sure you're devoting enough attention and energy to the things that are truly important to you.

THREE OF PENTAGRAMS

UPRIGHT: The Three of Pentagrams is a card of productive teamwork and collaboration. This tarot card suggests you'll achieve more success if you work with others toward a common goal rather than trying to do everything by yourself.

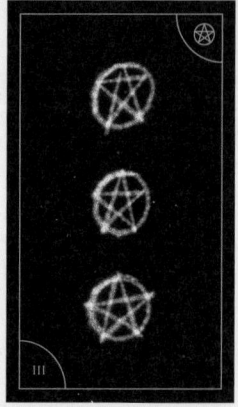

REVERSED: While the upright Three of Pentagrams represents productive, harmonious collaborations, its reversed orientation suggests a collaboration is struggling. This could be due to a communication breakdown, or your goals might not have enough clarity. To get things on track, take a step back, and review the current strategy with everyone involved to ensure you're all on the same page.

FOUR OF PENTAGRAMS

UPRIGHT: The Four of Pentagrams represents physical and financial security. This tarot card advises you to conserve your resources, and pay careful attention to your incoming and outgoing cash flow. Manage your income wisely, and beware of impulsive spending.

REVERSED: Bela Talbot is a skilled con artist, using lies to exploit and manipulate others to get what she wants from them. This sort of energy perfectly sums up the Four of Pentagrams reversed, which represents materialism, greed, and selfishness, particularly in regards to finances and material possessions. This tarot card serves as both a warning to make sure you're being treated fairly in situations regarding work and money and a reminder to treat others fairly in return.

FIVE OF PENTAGRAMS

UPRIGHT: The Five of Pentagrams tarot card suggests instability in your financial world or practical aspects of the home. Are you having trouble coming up with rent or your mortgage payment this month? Have you been caught off guard by an unexpected shift in your career? Focus on making sure your foundation is stable now.

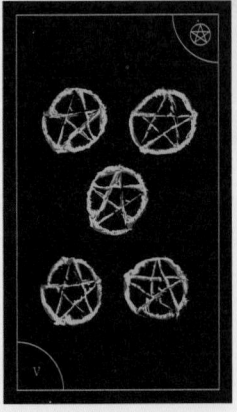

REVERSED: When reversed, the Five of Pentagrams indicates the foundational instability referenced by the upright Five of Pentagrams is ending. Hardships don't last forever. The reversed Five of Pentagrams comes as a sigh of relief, as it heralds the end of a difficult time.

SIX OF PENTAGRAMS

UPRIGHT: Balance and flow are the themes of the Six of Pentagrams tarot card. It indicates the exchange of wealth, reminding you to be charitable when you're in a position of abundance. Conversely, the Six of Pentagrams reminds you it's okay to ask for and accept help when you need it.

REVERSED: The Six of Pentagrams comes forward reversed in tarot readings when the flow of wealth in your life is out of balance. Do you have a lot of outstanding overdue debt? Are you continuing to feed into an investment that isn't showing you the returns you deserve? Take a careful look at your cash flow, and make adjustments accordingly.

SEVEN OF PENTAGRAMS

UPRIGHT: Arthur Ketch is an expert—if psycho-pathic—assassin whose illustrious position in the British Men of Letters is due to a long history of achieving hard results in his brutal work. He's a man who keeps his eye on the long game, even when it comes to planning for his own death. The Seven of Pentagrams is a reminder to remember the long game. Don't focus on getting instant results; instead, work hard to set yourself up for success.

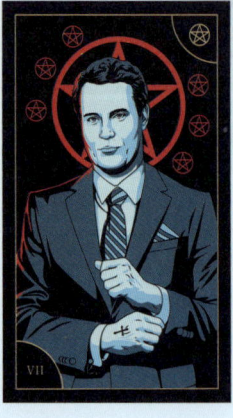

REVERSED: The Seven of Pentagrams reversed suggests a project relating to your finances won't be as successful as you anticipate. Even if there's brief instant gratification in this project, the long-term payout won't be very fruitful. Adjust your plans, and pivot as necessary.

EIGHT OF PENTAGRAMS

UPRIGHT: Jo Harvelle is a brave, independent woman who decided to follow in her father's footsteps and become a monster hunter, even though it means going against her mother's wishes. The Eight of Pentagrams suggests you embrace Jo's strong-willed spirit, and find your own career path. Don't let the naysayers hold you back; follow your passions and see where they lead.

REVERSED: The Eight of Pentagrams reversed indicates you're not spending your time and energy in the most productive ways. Are you putting a lot of effort into a project that isn't going anywhere? If you're working hard but still not seeing results, it might be time to move on.

NINE OF PENTAGRAMS

UPRIGHT: The Nine of Pentagrams indicates wealth, material abundance, healthy finances, and the satisfaction of living comfortably, knowing you have everything you need.

REVERSED: Material comforts and an abundance of money are great, but the Nine of Pentagrams reversed warns you not to let those things define you. Take care not to let your ego get wrapped up in your socioeconomic status or material possessions. Remember, you're worth more than what you own.

TEN OF PENTAGRAMS

UPRIGHT: Though he loves her and has the best of intentions, Dean complicates Lisa Braeden's life enormously. While he's in her life, she and her son, Ben, are in nearly constant danger of being attacked by supernatural monsters. Dean ultimately makes the decision to erase all of Lisa and Ben's memories of him, giving them the chance to have a happy, normal life together. The Ten of Pentagrams represents that happy, healthy home and stable family life—the kind of life the Winchesters, sadly, are unlikely to have.

REVERSED: While the upright Ten of Pentagrams indicates a happy, functional home, when the card is reversed, it signifies conflict at home, financial struggle, or major difficulties at work. Lisa Braeden and Dean love each other, but Dean's supernatural affiliations bring a lot of strife into their relationship. The Ten of Pentagrams reversed is indicative of this sort of chaos and uncertainty.

SUIT OF BLADES

KING OF BLADES

UPRIGHT: Cain notoriously
killed his brother Abel
with the First Blade and
became one of the most
feared and legendary
demons ever known. The
King of Blades represents a
powerful figure who
gained a strong reputation
through his actions over
time. This tarot card
advises you to lead with
intellect and logic, and to
rely on the knowledge and skill you've acquired
over the years to bring you to success.

KING OF BLADES

REVERSED: The King of Blades reversed represents a
figure much like Cain while he's under the influence of
the Mark of Cain: cold, unbalanced, and unconcerned
with others' feelings or the repercussions of their actions.
This tarot card is a sign to examine your relationship
with others. Treat people fairly, and make sure you're
behaving in ways that align with your moral compass.

QUEEN OF BLADES

UPRIGHT: High-ranking angel Naomi is a ruthless, complicated leader who, according to Castiel, fiercely cares about the safety and well-being of the souls in her charge—despite her unquestionably brutal methods. The Queen of Blades represents an intelligent, independent, protective figure. This tarot card advises you to be brave and unwavering in the pursuit of what you want. Stand your ground, muster your confidence, and know your worth.

QUEEN OF BLADES

REVERSED: When reversed, the Queen of Blades becomes manipulative, calculating, and self-serving—a side of Naomi that is on full display as she tortures and manipulates Castiel. This tarot card reminds you of the importance of having compassion for others and warns you not to try to bully others into getting your way.

KNIGHT OF BLADES

UPRIGHT: Abbadon is an intelligent, aggressive, and sadistic Knight of Hell who leads an uprising against Crowley upon discovering that "the salesman," as she calls him, has become King of Hell. The Knight of Blades represents an impulsive figure who steps in and takes action when others falter. If you find yourself stalling or putting something off, this tarot card advises you to act now.

KNIGHT OF BLADES

REVERSED: The Knight of Blades reversed suggests important information is being withheld. Some sort of vital communication isn't taking place. Whether you're the one holding back or someone's not being completely honest with you, the Knight of Blades reversed indicates communication issues need to be addressed.

PAGE OF BLADES

UPRIGHT: The Page of Blades represents an intelligent but inexperienced young person. Kevin Tran finds himself in over his head as he becomes suddenly embroiled in the supernatural world as a prophet of God. The Page of Blades advises you to recognize both your talent and skill while acknowledging when you need help or guidance.

PAGE OF BLADES

REVERSED: The Page of Blades represents a figure much like Kevin Tran in the apocalypse world, who reluctantly uses his gifts to help the archangel Michael devestate that world. Though Kevin feels like he doesn't have a choice and needs to help Michael to get into Heaven, he causes a lot of damage. This tarot card reversed advises you to recognize the potential consequences of your actions and to really think through things rather than making impulsive decisions.

ACE OF BLADES

UPRIGHT: The First Blade was notoriously used by Cain to commit humanity's first murder. The Ace of Blades represents power, creation and destruction, decisive action, and breakthroughs. This tarot card advises you to use your skills and intellect wisely, because you're more powerful than you realize.

ACE OF BLADES

REVERSED: The Ace of Blades reversed represents reckless decisions, confusion, and poor judgment. Now isn't the time to let emotions cloud your thinking. Clear your head, and make sure you're seeing things from a logical perspective to avoid regret.

TWO OF BLADES

UPRIGHT: The Two of Blades represents a tough decision to be made, particularly in regards to your beliefs, convictions, and moral compass. This card advises you to stay true to yourself.

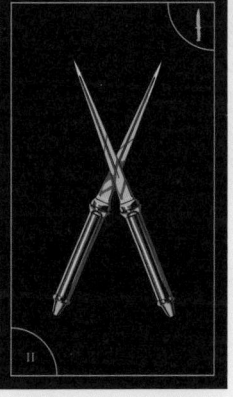

REVERSED: The Two of Blades reversed represents stalling tactics, indecision, and deadlock. If you've been in a debate or a big discussion with someone that just isn't productive, it may be time to let bygones be bygones. Sometimes compromises and common ground just can't be found.

THREE OF BLADES

UPRIGHT: Madison's story is
a tale of tragedy and heart-
break, which are major
themes of the Three of
Blades. Madison was the
victim of a werewolf bite,
and though she and the
hunters searched desper-
ately for a cure, she
ultimately realized she
would always be dangerous
and chose to sacrifice
herself to save others. The
Three of Blades symbolizes
loss, sorrow, and sometimes, betrayal.

REVERSED: The heartache represented by the upright
Three of Blades begins to mend. This tarot card
reversed symbolizes the process of healing from old
wounds and loss. Be gentle with yourself, and let yourself feel what you need to feel. You'll get through this.

FOUR OF BLADES

UPRIGHT: The Four of Blades suggests it's time for some hard-earned rest and relaxation. You're coming out of a difficult period in your life, and it's time to take a break and allow yourself to process recent events.

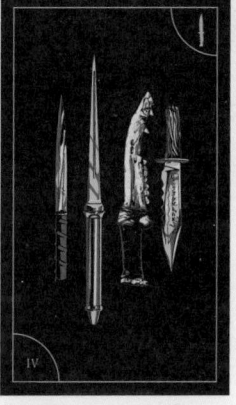

REVERSED: When reversed, the Four of Blades tarot card represents the deep exhaustion and burnout that comes when we don't give ourselves the rest we require. You've been fighting hard for a long time and feel as though you have nothing left to give. The Four of Blades suggests you take a moment to rest and gather your strength before carrying on. The end is in sight. Give yourself one last break before the final push.

FIVE OF BLADES

UPRIGHT: From the moment the brothers meet demon Meg Masters, she causes trouble for them. While she eventually becomes a sort of ally to the team, her presence is almost always a source of discord and tension. The Five of Blades is the ultimate conflict card. It symbolizes battles, changes, and fierce disagreements. This tarot card shows you're dealing with a lot of unrest, but keep going, the end of this fight is in sight!

REVERSED: The conflicted energy of the upright Five of Blades turns inward. You're struggling with something internally. Whether something isn't sitting right with your moral compass or you're wrestling with a tough decision, if you're feeling overwhelmed, it might be time to take a step back and stop thinking about the situation for a little while. Thinking yourself into confusion and getting upset won't help you.

SIX OF BLADES

UPRIGHT: The Six of Blades represents the period of rest that follows a struggle. It's a reprieve, a sigh, a laying down of swords. This tarot card marks a transition from a chaotic phase into a calmer one. Sometimes, this card indicates actual travel.

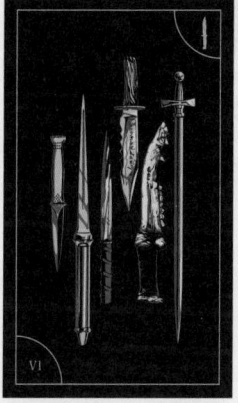

REVERSED: The Six of Blades reversed indicates you're going through a transition but are experiencing delays. These bumps in the road can relate to actual travel setbacks, or they can refer to small setbacks in a personal journey. If you've hit a few roadblocks, don't be discouraged. Persevere, because you're sure to get there in the end.

SEVEN OF BLADES

UPRIGHT: From the
moment the Winchesters
meet demon Ruby, it's clear
she's up to no good. Ruby
masterfully seduces and
manipulates Sam, hooking
him on demon blood and
eventually convincing him
to kill Lilith, thus releasing
Lucifer from the Cage and
starting the apocalypse.
The Seven of Blades
indicates sneaky behavior
and betrayal. This tarot

card advises you to stay vigilant and listen to your
instincts. If you get the feeling someone's not being
entirely honest with you, trust yourself, and investigate
the situation further.

REVERSED: While the upright Seven of Blades indicates
lying and trickery, reversed, this tarot card suggests
you're not being honest with yourself. Is there a
personal truth you're not letting yourself acknowledge?
The Seven of Blades reversed indicates lying to yourself
will only cause you grief. Being honest is the only way
to grow and move forward.

EIGHT OF BLADES

UPRIGHT: Constance Welch is a ghost who gets men to drive her to her former house then murders them after tempting them into unfaithfulness. Like many ghosts, she is unable to move on, trapped between life and death by her unwillingness to face the truth of her situation. The Eight of Blades indicates feelings of imprisonment, restriction, and a victim mentality. Though you may feel powerless and victimized, you actually have a lot of control over the situation. Accept the responsibility for your own fate, and you will free yourself.

REVERSED: The Eight of Blades reversed represents self-deprecation and criticizing. If you've recently lost your confidence, it may be that you've been bullying yourself. Have you become your own worst enemy? Give yourself a break, and be kind to yourself. You're doing your best.

NINE OF BLADES

UPRIGHT: Alistair is a
particularly nasty demon,
and Hell's Grand Inquisitor.
He has a particular affinity
for torturing victims not
only physically but psycho-
logically and emotionally.
The Nine of Blades is a
tarot card of anxiety, night-
mares, and worry. It
indicates stress and
suggests you need to make
time to consciously relax.

REVERSED: If you've recently started taking steps to
overcome stressors in your life and create more balance,
the reversed Nine of Blades is a positive sign that this
was a good move and that you're beginning to heal.
This tarot card indicates the feelings of being overwhelmed by grief, worry, stress, or anxiety are coming
to an end. Don't let Alistair win; this period of your life
will wind down soon.

TEN OF BLADES

UPRIGHT: Adam Milligan's life is filled with painful twists of fate. After growing up thinking he's an only child, Adam discovers he has half brothers, Sam and Dean, and is swept into their dark, complicated supernatural world. Eventually, he's even sealed into Lucifer's Cage along with Michael, Sam, and Lucifer.

The Ten of Blades represents a dramatic turn of events and advises you to stay on your toes and expect the unexpected, because you never know what fate has in store for you.

REVERSED: The Ten of Blades reversed represents regret and betrayal—such as being sacrificed and forgotten by your half brothers. The Ten of Blades reversed reminds you that you will ultimately find your way out of this complicated situation, even when all seems hopeless. Be brave, and don't despair.

SUIT OF GOBLETS

KING OF GOBLETS

UPRIGHT: The Alpha Vampire creates an enormous, lasting legacy of vampires, whom he considers his children and cares for deeply. The King of Goblets represents a caring, patriarchal figure. This tarot card advises you to treat others with kindness and to approach challenges with tact and diplomacy.

KING OF GOBLETS

REVERSED: The King of Goblets reversed represents someone who's prone to unpredictable emotional outbursts. He can be manipulative and knows how to exploit others' compassion for personal gain. If you've been dealing with someone prone to this sort of volatility, this tarot card cautions you to be wary of them. Take what they say with a grain of salt, and keep your guard up.

QUEEN OF GOBLETS

UPRIGHT: The Queen of Goblets is a nurturing but tough matriarchal figure, much like hunter, mother, and saloon owner Ellen Harvelle. Ellen is very protective of her daughter, Jo; this sort of caring, fierce mother-bear energy perfectly represents the Queen of Goblets. This tarot card is a reminder to be nurturing and compassionate with those you love.

QUEEN OF GOBLETS

REVERSED: The Queen of Goblets reversed loses control of her emotions, becoming dramatic and emotionally toxic. Have you been letting your emotions get the better of you? If so, recognize the consequences of your actions, and do what you need to do to regain balance and stability.

KNIGHT OF GOBLETS

UPRIGHT: The Knight of Goblets is considered the archetypal Knight in Shining Armor tarot card. It represents someone like Garth Fitzgerald IV, who is a compassionate, caring, emotionally intelligent sweetheart. This tarot card suggests you spend time nurturing your close connections with others. Whether they're friends,

KNIGHT OF GOBLETS

family, or romantic partners, let the people close to you know how much you care about and appreciate them.

REVERSED: The Knight of Goblets reversed represents someone with brooding, jealous, spiteful energy. If you're dealing with someone who's become demanding or who gaslights you, take a step back and be firm about your boundaries. The Knight of Goblets reversed is known for crossing them.

PAGE OF GOBLETS

UPRIGHT: The Page of Goblets represents a dreamer who's fueled by their own curiosity, like superfan Becky Rosen. Becky gets swept up in her romantic fantasies and sometimes loses sight of reality. The Page of Goblets tarot card advises you to keep dreaming big, but make sure your feet are on the ground. Sometimes this card heralds the start of a new close friendship or relationship.

PAGE OF GOBLETS

REVERSED: The Page of Goblets reversed represents someone who's having a lot of difficulty connecting with their emotions and expressing them. It's time to get in touch with your feelings. Don't be afraid to be emotionally vulnerable with those you love—that's how deeper connections are formed.

ACE OF GOBLETS

UPRIGHT: The Ace of Goblets represents an overflowing of positive feelings—often the warm and happy beginnings of a new relationship or friendship. This card advises you to appreciate new connections in your life, because you will come to find them emotionally fulfilling.

ACE OF GOBLETS

REVERSED: The Ace of Goblets reversed indicates you aren't exercising control over your emotions. They're bursting out of you in unhealthy ways. Expressing yourself is one thing, but be careful not to let yourself become irrational and overly emotional to your own detriment.

TWO OF GOBLETS

UPRIGHT: Though they have their differences, Bobby and Rufus are long-standing partners, friends, and allies in the war against the supernatural. This sort of close bond is represented by the Two of Goblets tarot card. It suggests a harmonious and mutually beneficial partnership, friendship, or relationship.

REVERSED: When reversed, the Two of Goblets tarot card indicates a partnership in your life is no longer in sync. Whether you're not seeing eye to eye with a close friend, family member, or partner, or perhaps you blame them for the death of someone you loved, the Two of Goblets reversed shows there are major clashes going on within a relationship. Communicate honestly and openly to try to get on the same page again.

THREE OF GOBLETS

UPRIGHT: The Three of Goblets represents an intimate bond, friendship, and collaboration. When this tarot card appears in a reading, take it as a sign to connect with your loved ones, and let them know how much you appreciate them.

REVERSED: The Three of Goblets reversed represents a crowding or stifling experience, especially relating to close personal relationships. Sometimes, this tarot card can represent unfaithfulness or even a love triangle.

FOUR OF GOBLETS

UPRIGHT: After Donatello loses his soul, he loses his joie de vivre. His lack of a moral compass makes him apathetic and uncaring. The Four of Goblets represents boredom and apathy. This tarot card advises you to reconnect with things that inspire you to reignite your spark.

REVERSED: The Four of Goblets reversed represents the feeling of getting your spark back. If you find yourself feeling lost or unsure of how to move forward, the Four of Goblets reversed suggests a new path to fulfillment will soon be revealed to you.

FIVE OF GOBLETS

UPRIGHT: The Five of Goblets represents a great failure or loss. Gadreel was tasked with guarding the Garden of Eden from evil. He ultimately failed, which led to the corruption of mankind. Gadreel is racked with guilt for having failed to protect the Garden of Eden. The Five of Goblets advises you to learn from your mistakes, then move on.

REVERSED: The Five of Goblets reversed suggests you're fighting an emotional internal struggle. It could be that you're trying to ignore and conceal your emotions, to your own detriment. You need to allow yourself to process your feelings before you can move on from them.

SIX OF GOBLETS

UPRIGHT: The Six of Goblets is a call to reconnect with pure, unbridled joy. When's the last time you did something silly or unexpected, just because it made you happy? The Six of Goblets tarot card suggests life has been feeling heavy lately. It's time to get out of the doldrums by doing things that genuinely make you happy, whether that means making music, painting, or simply eating a slice of warm apple pie.

REVERSED: The Six of Goblets reversed indicates you're getting too caught up in the past. Reminiscing can be fun and healthy if it's done occasionally, but be careful not to get so swept up in remembering the past that you fail to live in the present.

SEVEN OF GOBLETS

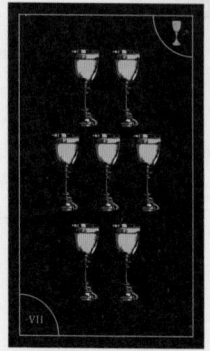

UPRIGHT: The Seven of Goblets advises you to keep a grounded perspective when faced with mulitple opportunities or choices. Grand visions and goals are great, but be careful not to get so caught up in dreams and fantasies that you end up getting yourself into trouble. Now is the time to focus on one thing. Choose wisely.

REVERSED: When reversed, the Seven of Goblets tarot card indicates an unfocused, scattered state of mind. Are you sure you're seeing things as they are? If you're having some trouble getting clarity on a situation, take a step away to center yourself. When you calm down and focus, you'll be able to approach things with a much more level head.

EIGHT OF GOBLETS

UPRIGHT: Angel Anna Milton gives up her grace to become human, having become disillusioned and disappointed with her life as a soldier in the heavenly host. If you're feeling lost or aimless, have hope: Just as Anna chooses to experience humanity, you too can choose to pursue a path that brings you joy and fulfillment. Allow yourself to dream now. Later, those dreams will turn into goals, and your passion will reignite as you work hard to achieve them.

REVERSED: After discovering her true identity as an angel, Anna Milton makes the reluctant decision to reabsorb her grace in order to protect herself from the angels and demons chasing her. The Eight of Goblets reversed represents a tough decision, which results in a departure. If you're feeling stuck in an emotional situation, friendship, or relationship, it might be time to cut ties and move on.

NINE OF GOBLETS

UPRIGHT: The Nine of Goblets represents deep emotional fulfillment. This tarot card symbolizes happiness, satisfaction, and getting what you want. When the Nine of Goblets is drawn in a reading, it advises you to have faith in your dreams, because fate is conspiring to make them come true.

REVERSED: When reversed, the Nine of Goblets tarot card indicates dissatisfaction or a lack of fulfillment. Have you been wishing hard for something, only to have your dreams not come to fruition? The Nine of Goblets reversed reminds you some things just aren't meant to be.

TEN OF GOBLETS

UPRIGHT: The Ten of Goblets represents happy, harmonious relationships and a healthy emotional balance. This tarot card suggests you're entering a period of deep emotional fulfillment when you will feel supported and valued by friends and family. The Ten of Goblets tarot card advises you to cherish your loved ones and enjoy the moment.

REVERSED: The Ten of Goblets reversed suggests you're enduring struggles within interpersonal relationships. Has there been conflict in your home? Have you been at odds with a close friend? It's time to get to the bottom of these conflicts and work on resolving them before they get out of hand and lead to heartache.

TAROT
READINGS

The practice of tarot reading is highly customizable, so you can experiment with different methods until you find what works best for you. There are many fabled "rules" surrounding tarot. For example, some people say readings should only occur on full moons, while others create complex rituals around it. The truth is that tarot reading has no rules, and that's the beauty of it. Read tarot however often or infrequently you'd like; make it a sacred, ritualistic practice, or approach it from a more casual or secular point of view; bring crystals into your tarot reading space, or take your deck out with friends.

CARING FOR YOUR DECK

Energetically cleansing your tarot deck between readings will ensure it's always fresh and ready to give you clear, accurate readings. In *Supernatural*, salt is commonly used in purification and cleansing. So, similarly, you can use salt to energetically purify your tarot deck. Store your deck in the center of a ring of salt to cleanse and protect its energy. Alternatively, you can achieve the same results by passing the tarot deck through the smoke of smoldering sage or palo santo, or by leaving it in moonlight overnight. The crystal selenite is also known for cleansing; place selenite atop your deck when it's not in use, and your deck will be refreshed and ready for you when you return to it.

METHODS FOR READING TAROT

Before beginning a tarot reading, start by formulating a question. Feel free to ask the cards anything: How do I progress in my career? What dynamics in my relationship need to be worked on? Will Sam remember to get pie? Tarot readings can give you insight and advice about any situation, predicament, interpersonal connection, or decision you find yourself faced with.

Some people like to meditate before tarot readings, or relax by taking a bath. Whatever method you use, clearing your head will help you get a clearer reading. When you feel ready, ask your cards a question, then shuffle them. There's no correct or incorrect way to shuffle. Some tarot readers like to shuffle them like playing cards, while others use an overhand shuffle to avoid bending them. You can even spread the deck out in front of you and mix them up by hand.

After you've asked your question and shuffled the deck, it's time to draw cards, and lay them out in a tarot spread. Tarot spreads are the specific ways cards are arranged after they've been drawn from a deck. Each card placement has an individual meaning unique to the spread. Here are a few tarot spreads to get you started on your tarot journey.

THE SPREADS

APPLE PIE TAROT SPREAD

It's no secret that Dean Winchester absolutely loves pie.
Though he comes close to eating it so many times, his
attempts are often unluckily thwarted in one way or
another. This tarot spread is designed to help you
discover what it is you really want out of life—and how
to get it. Dean accuses Sam of wanting a conventional,
apple-pie life free of the perils and complications of
monster hunting. Whether you'd like an apple-pie life of
your own, or your heart's desires are more adventurous,
this tarot spread will reveal your truth.

CARD 1. THE PRESENT

This card is representative of the overall theme of this current chapter of your life. It's the starting point on your journey to the goal shown by The Apple Pie card.

CARD 2. THE APPLE PIE

What will truly fulfill you? Pay careful attention to the suit of the tarot card drawn for this placement. If it's a Goblets card, your goal involves emotions and personal connections. If the card is Blades, your goal relates to the mind, knowledge, or making big changes. A Pentagrams card indicates your desires involve your home life, career, possessions, or other aspects of the physical realm and your relationship to it. A card of the Bones suit shows your goals involve creative expression and inspiration.

CARD 3. THE OBSTACLE

What obstacles are holding you back? This card placement reveals the behaviors, beliefs, or obstacles currently preventing you from achieving your goal.

CARD 4. THE ACTION

This card placement shows what action you can take right now to start turning the dream revealed by The Apple Pie tarot card into your reality.

LUCIFER'S CAGE TAROT SPREAD

Lucifer's Cage is a notorious prison that has held some of the most powerful supernatural beings in existence. This tarot spread is designed to show you what's caging you—in other words, what's holding you back from reaching your potential. This spread will show you how to work through those obstacles so you can live your happiest, most fulfilled life.

1 **2** **3**

CARD 1. THE CAGE

This tarot card reveals what behaviors, actions, or situations are holding you back.

CARD 2. THE SEAL

Just as Lucifer's Cage is locked using 66 Seals that need to be broken in order to open the Cage, this tarot card reveals the action that needs to be taken in order for you to overcome the obstacle represented by The Cage card.

CARD 3. BREAKING THE SEAL

This tarot card represents what will happen when you take the action revealed by The Seal card and free yourself from your own personal cage.

TEAM FREE WILL TAROT SPREAD

This is a great tarot spread to use when you're faced with a difficult decision and you'd like more insight into the true nature of your choices and their possible outcomes. This tarot spread may have been helpful for Sam when he was deciding whether or not to allow Lucifer to possess him. On the one hand, it could've led to the apocalypse; on the other, it gave them their best chance of defeating him. This tarot spread is designed to help you make decisions by giving you clarity. As Dean Winchester says, "You always have a choice."

CARD 1. OPTION A

This tarot card gives you clarity by representing the true nature of the first option you're considering.

CARD 2. OPTION B

This tarot card represents the true nature of the second option you're considering.

CARD 3. EFFECTS OF OPTION A

This card shows the likely outcome if you decide on the option represented by Card 1.

CARD 4. EFFECTS OF OPTION B

This card shows the likely outcome if you decide on the option represented by Card 2.

CARD 5. ADVICE

This tarot card gives you important warnings or advice you need to keep in mind while making your final decision.

ABOUT THE AUTHOR

MINERVA SIEGEL is the author of *Tarot for Self-Care: How to Use Tarot to Manifest Your Best Self.* She writes about subjects such as tarot, witchcraft, and living with disabilities for both print magazines and large online publications like Elite Daily. She has been a guest on podcasts such as *The Queer Witch Podcast* and *The Now Age Podcast* with Ruby Warrington. When not writing, she spends her days practicing divination and drinking rose lattes in the Victorian house she shares with her husband and their rescued pack of misfit dogs. You can find her on Instagram using her online handle @SpookyFatBabe.

ABOUT THE ILLUSTRATOR

MATTHEW SKIFF is an illustrator who has worked with a number of properties and clients, including *Ghostbusters*, *Alien*, and *RoboCop*. Outside of that, he has spent a significant amount of time designing art for the skateboard industry, creating art prints for various galleries, and most recently, creating art for action figures and their packaging. You can find out more about his work by visiting matthewskiff.com.

TITAN
BOOKS

144 Southwark Street
London, SE1 0UP
www.titanbooks.com

 Find us on Facebook: www.facebook.com/titanbooks
Follow us on Twitter: @TitanBooks

Published by arrangement with Insight Editions,
PO Box 3088, San Rafael, CA 94912 USA
www.insighteditions.com

A CIP Catalogue record for this title is available from the British
Library.

ISBN: 978-1-78909-757-3

ROOTS of PEACE REPLANTED PAPER

Manufactured in China by Insight Editions

10 9 8 7 6 5 4 3